W9-CLL-209

Small Blessings

A Book of Prayers for Children

WRITTEN AND COMPILED BY

DON HARP

ILLUSTRATED BY

DANIEL GILL

LONGSTREET PRESS

Atlanta

Published by
LONGSTREET PRESS, INC.
2140 Newmarket Parkway
Suite 122
Marietta, GA 30067

Copyright © 2001 by Donald Harp
Illustrations Copyright © 2001 by Daniel Gill

All rights reserved. No part of this book may be reproduced in any
form or by any means without the prior written permission of the
Publisher, excepting brief quotations used in connection with reviews,
written specifically for inclusion in a magazine or newspaper.

Printed in the United States of America

1st printing 2001

Library of Congress Catalog Card Number: 00-111982

ISBN: 1-56352-650-6

Jacket and book design by Burtch Bennett Hunter
Edited by Tysie Whitman and Ann Lovett

A Preface for Parents

Frequently I am asked the question "How do I teach my child to pray?" It was a request made of Jesus by the disciples: "Master, teach us to pray." It is a question I suspect is on the minds of many adults, as well.

Teaching children to pray for needs instead of wants is a fundamental of prayer. Their lives begin with their needs being met; food, clothing, warmth, and love are provided by their parents. As they grow older, needs are often replaced by wants. The secret to a healthy prayer life begins early by teaching, both by word and example, to pray for needs.

Always teach your child to give thanks first, for gratitude is the parent of all virtues. The ability to say thank you will serve your child throughout his or her life. Teach your child the value of praying for others as well as self. A good place to begin is to pray for family, friends, teachers, and those with special needs, such as the poor and the sick.

I hope that the examples in this little book will be helpful in teaching your children to pray.

∽ Don Harp

Dedicated to the memory of
Eva Blanche Harp
and Doris Anna Harp,
my paternal grandmother and mother,
who taught me to pray.

For He will give His angels charge of you
to guard you in all your ways.

~ *Psalms 91:11 RSV*

Table of Contents

∽ ∾

Prayers for Every Mood
page 9

∽ ∾

Everyday Prayers
page 19

∽ ∾

Prayers for Special Occasions
page 37

Small Blessings

Prayers for Every Mood

Thank You for each happy day,
For fun, for friends,
And work and play;
Thank You for Your loving care,
Here at home and everywhere.
Amen.

Dear God,
I am so happy today.
Thank You for helping me feel this way.
In my heart I want to say
Thank You for joy on this day.
Amen.

Please give me what I ask, dear Lord,
If You'd be glad about it.
But if You think it's not for me,
Please help me do without it.
Amen.

When I despise myself or the world,
Let me find Your image within me again.
Blessed are You, O Lord,
Who have made me as You wanted me.
Amen.

Dear God,
There are days when I feel sad.
Some of those days I have been bad,
But other days I just feel blue.
Please help me learn to turn to You.
Amen.

"What God Hath Promised"

God hath not promised skies always blue,
Flower-strewn pathways
all our lives through.
God hath not promised sun without rain,
Joy without sorrow, peace without pain.

But God hath promised strength for the day,
Rest for the labor, light for the way,
Grace for the trials, help from above,
Unfailing sympathy, undying love.

cᴏ Annie Johnson Flint

When I am sick and cannot play
Lord, be with me on that day.
Keep me cheerful, and brave, too,
Remembering other children who
Are also ill, perhaps in pain,
Lord, help us all to health again.

J.W.A.

Everyday Prayers

Now another day is breaking,
Sleep was sweet and so is waking,
Dear Lord, I promised You last night
Never again to sulk or fight.
Such vows are easier to keep
When a child is sound asleep.
Today, O Lord, for Your dear sake,
I'll try to keep them when awake.

✍ *Ogden Nash*

I thank thee, Lord, for sleep and rest,
For all the things that I love best.
Now guide me through another day
And bless my work and bless my play.
Amen.

Now, *before I run to play,*
Let me not forget to pray
To God who kept me through the night
And waked me with the morning light.
Amen.

cᴓ ᴓꜱ

Dear God,
Help me this day to give away a smile,
Help me be a friend to another child.
Teach me the value of doing what's right,
Be present in me and keep me in Your sight.
Amen.

Thank You for my friend next door,
And my friend across the street,
And please help me to be a friend
To everyone I meet.
Amen.

Lord, teach a little child to pray
And then accept my prayer.
I know You hear the words I say
For You are everywhere.
Teach me to do the thing that's right,
And when I'm wrong, forgive,
And make me willing day and night
To serve You while I live.

✆ *Jane Taylor*

The light of God before me
The light of God behind me
The light of God above me
The light of God beside me
The light of God within me.

Prayer of St. Patrick

God is great, God is good,
Let us thank Him for this food.
By His hands we all are fed
Give us, Lord, our daily bread.
Amen.

Father, we thank Thee for this food,
For health and strength and all things good.
May others all these blessings share,
And hearts be grateful everywhere.
Amen.

Be present at our table, Lord,
Be here and everywhere adored;
Thy mercies bless and grant that we
May feast in fellowship with Thee.

Blessing of John Wesley

Thank You for the world so sweet,
Thank You for the food we eat,
Thank You for the birds that sing,
Thank You, God, for everything.

∽ *Edith Rutter Leatham*

Dear God,
As we sit with food and drink,
We offer thanks when we think
That of all Your gifts from above
The best one of them is Your love.
Amen.

*Now I lay me down to sleep
I pray the Lord my soul to keep
If I should die before I wake
I pray the Lord my soul to take.
Amen.*

Matthew, Mark, Luke, and John,
Bless the bed I lie upon.
Four corners to my bed,
Four angels round my head,
One to watch and one to pray
And two to keep all harm away.
Amen.

＊

Time has come for me to sleep
And I thank Thee for Thy keep.
Watch this night well over me
Teach me, Lord, to trust in Thee.

Many sins I've done today
Please, Lord, take them all away.
Look upon me in Thy grace
Make me pure before Thy face.

Care for children sick and poor
Grant them, Lord, Thy blessing more.
Care for Mom and Dad the same
This I pray in Jesus's name.

For food and clothes and toys and such,
We thank You, Lord, so very much.
And when it's time for us to sleep,
We ask You, Lord, our souls to keep.
Amen.

Prayers for Special Occasions

∽⊙ ⊙∽

The Lord's Prayer

Our Father, who art in Heaven
Hallowed be Thy name.
Thy kingdom come,
Thy will be done,
On earth as it is in Heaven.

Give us this day our daily bread
And forgive us our trespasses,
As we forgive those who trespass against us.

And lead us not into temptation,
But deliver us from evil.
For Thine is the kingdom,
And the power, and the glory
Forever and ever.
Amen.

cᴓ ᏝᏙ

O Jesus, shed Thy tender love
upon me, please, today.
On this birthday give me grace,
my special prayer to say.
Few are my candles, few my years;
so let my promise be
That all the years that I may live
I'll love and worship Thee.

The year has turned its circle,
The seasons come and go.
The harvest all is gathered in
And chilly north winds blow.
Orchards have shared their treasures,
The fields, their yellow grain,
So open wide the doorway —
Thanksgiving comes again!

"We Plow the Fields"

We plow the fields, and scatter
the good seed on the land,
But it is fed and watered
by God's almighty hand;
He sends the snow in winter,
the warmth to swell the grain,
The breezes and the sunshine,
and soft refreshing rain.

We thank Thee, then, O Father,
for all things bright and good,
The seed time and the harvest,
our life, our health, and food;
No gifts have we to offer,
for all Thy love imparts,
But that which Thou desirest,
our humble, thankful hearts.

☙ ❧

Dear God,
In this holiday season of gladness and joy,
Help me be a generous and better boy.
Amen.

☙ ❧

Dear God,
In this holiday season of giving and whirl,
Help me be a kind and thoughtful girl.
Amen.

Now we'll stay awake and
make our house clean
With the brightest things of red and green.
And we'll wait for Jesus until He comes,
We'll wait until He comes.

First we'll put up a tree
all shiny and bright,
With lights and balls
to shine through the night.
Then build Him a house
with a little bed,
A place high enough
not to bump His head.

Bring sheep and shepherds
to see Him newborn,
And a cow and a donkey
to keep Him warm.
O good Lord Jesus, asleep in the hay,
Bless all little children
each night and each day.